Crafted from Nature:
Rustic Furniture Techniques

Bim Willow

Schiffer Publishing Ltd®

4880 Lower Valley Road · Atglen, Pennsylvania 19310

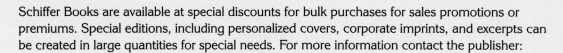

Schiffer Books are available at special discounts for bulk purchases for sales promotions or premiums. Special editions, including personalized covers, corporate imprints, and excerpts can be created in large quantities for special needs. For more information contact the publisher:

Published by Schiffer Publishing Ltd.
4880 Lower Valley Road
Atglen, PA 19310
Phone: (610) 593-1777; Fax: (610) 593-2002
E-mail: Info@schifferbooks.com

For the largest selection of fine reference books on this and related subjects, please visit our web site at **www.schifferbooks.com**
We are always looking for people to write books on new and related subjects. If you have an idea for a book please contact us at the above address.

This book may be purchased from the publisher.
Include $5.00 for shipping.
Please try your bookstore first.
You may write for a free catalog.

In Europe, Schiffer books are distributed by
Bushwood Books
6 Marksbury Ave.
Kew Gardens
Surrey TW9 4JF England
Phone: 44 (0) 20 8392 8585; Fax: 44 (0) 20 8392 9876
E-mail: info@bushwoodbooks.co.uk
Website: www.bushwoodbooks.co.uk

Copyright © 2010 by Lawrence Schackow
Library of Congress Control Number: 2010930820

All rights reserved. No part of this work may be reproduced or used in any form or by any means—graphic, electronic, or mechanical, including photocopying or information storage and retrieval systems—without written permission from the publisher.

The scanning, uploading and distribution of this book or any part thereof via the Internet or via any other means without the permission of the publisher is illegal and punishable by law. Please purchase only authorized editions and do not participate in or encourage the electronic piracy of copyrighted materials.

"Schiffer," "Schiffer Publishing Ltd. & Design," and the "Design of pen and inkwell" are registered trademarks of Schiffer Publishing Ltd.

Designed by RoS
Type set in Tiza/Korinna BT
ISBN: 978-0-7643-3326-2
Printed in China

Contents

Introduction

There were simpler times when men and women created things for their utility and enjoyment — tools, toys, clothing, and other primitive works, including rustic furniture. For some this basic furniture making craft evolved into a more sophisticated art form, now known as refined rustic. This paradoxical adaptation took place around 1900 when rustic furniture was in its heyday. In recent years, there has been a renewed demand for rustic and refined rustic for both homes and gardens, as well an interest in how it is made. As our world becomes more packaged and processed, it seems that people yearn for more of nature in their lives.

Each of the three women in this book has developed a different and very personal refined rustic art form. With pictures and concise instructions, they demonstrate their techniques so that you too can create a rustic treasure to cherish for years to come.

I am proud to present to you the works of Skye Gregson, Jane Voorhees, and Marcia Perry.

A Birch Bark Frame

Jane was born in 1951 and grew up in the New York Metropolitan area. She studied at Eastern Michigan University, the school of visual arts, and received a B. A. from Livingston College at the Rutgers University. Her supplemental education was in the form of an apprenticeship to jeweler Paula Gollhardt, enameling with Bill Helwig, and jewelry workshops with Chuck Evans, Rick Marshall, Marci Zelmanoff, and Mary Ann Scheer.

She studied painting at the Montclair Art Museum and had five years of pastel and portraiture at the Yard School of Art under Margaret Yard Tyler from 1975 -1977. She ran the wax production and the setup room for the jewelry casting firm of Century Casting in New York City.

Jane has been producing her own line of jewelry from 1975 to the present. In 1990 she pursued her long admiration for rustic motifs and began making furniture, frames, and accessories. She continues to paint in pastels and add to her fine jewelry line.

The project is an 8-1/2" x 10-1/2"" frame with a 4" x 6" opening. The base frame is 1" x 3" lumber. 2 pieces, 3-5/8" x 2-1/2"; 2 pieces 10-1/2" x 2-1/2". The rabbets are created with 1/4" strips.

The corners are butt-fit and screwed together. The rabbets are cut to the fit the opening.

The rabbet is attached to the frame so it is flush with the front edge…

…giving a lip to support the glass or mirror.

Blacken the outside of the frame where it will be covered with bark. This keeps the wood from showing through.

If the frame is to be used for a mirror, the inside of the rabbet is also colored black so the wood will not reflect in the mirror.

With the frame face down, trace around it on tracing paper.

The result.

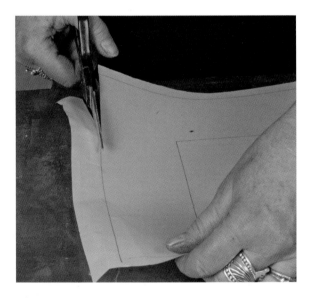

Cut out the pattern...

...and make the opening.

Lay the pattern on the face of the frame to draw the design on it. I start by drawing the quadrants. I use a straight edge to carry the lines of the opening to the edge of the frame.

Mark the grain directions that you wish to see in the finished frame.

After the grain direction is drawn cut out the three different sections (They are used twice or four times to make the eight sections.)

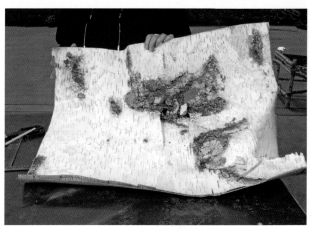

This large piece of birch bark is the basis of the decoration on the frame. I use standing dead trees or trees that are being taken for a construction project. Never ring a tree of its bark…it will kill the tree. I harvest the bark in the spring because the bark comes right off. In the fall it is very difficult to remove the bark from the tree.

In addition to the ease of bark removal, the colors of the bark are great in the spring.

The inner cambium will maintain this color. This piece has been off the tree for 4 years and the color is still great. You can store bark indefinitely if you keep it flat and dry.

The bark will separate into different layers each with its own color.

The tracing paper patterns allow you to see the grain and align the arrow to it.

Starting with the corner piece of the frame, I line the arrow up with the grain of the bark...

...trace the pattern...

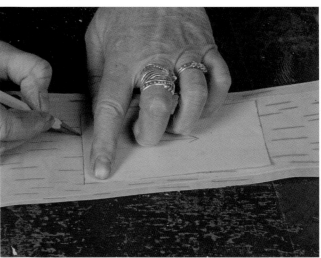

...and cut it out. Repeat for all four corners.

The same process is used on longer side panels. Lay the pattern so the arrow follows the grain of the bark, trace it, and cut it out.

Do the same for the shorter top pieces.

The surface pieces all cut.

The outside edge of the frame is trimmed with twigs. The twig needs to be as thick as the frame edge. Fit the twig so the straightest edge is against the frame.

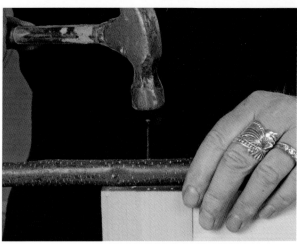

Begin with the top and bottom edges. Secure the twig to the edge with panel nails.

Trim the top and bottom twigs flush with the edge of the frame. My saw blade is running next to the edge of the frame.

Line up the twigs for the sides of the frame.

Nail them in place and cut flush with the top and bottom twigs.

Lay out the bark to check the fit.

Turn the pieces off the frame so their back sides are facing up.,

I use contact cement to hold the bark in place while I work. Apply the glue to the back of the bark…

…and to the surface of the frame. Let it dry.

When the glue has dried, align the bark with the outside edge of the frame…

…and pat in place. Gaps will be covered and overlaps into the opening will be taken care of later.

Continue applying the bark around the frame.

When all the bark is in place, run a blade around the edge of the opening and slice off the excess.

Touch up the black color on the inside of the opening.

The edge of the opening is lined with twigs. Measure the length..

...and cut it.

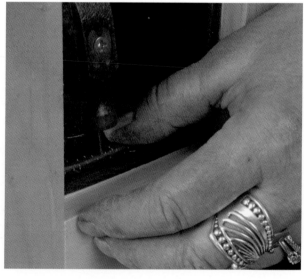

Hold it in place...

...and nail it with brass brads.

Progress.

A thinner twig acts as the inner trim piece and is added to the edge of the frame. The top and bottom pieces should extend a bit beyond the bark.

The brass brads now become part of the decoration, so I think about where I will put them. I'm going to put one in the middle of each panel.

You also have to think about securing the trim, so I am adding another brad here where there is a slight bend in the twig. I will put a matching brad at the other side to keep the symmetry of the design.

Match the pattern on the other side of the frame.

The end pieces butt-fit against the side pieces, which is the reason for cutting them long.

Progress.

Add separating trim between the segments. Start with the long lines.

Continue with cross pieces.

Progress.

The decoration of the corners uses thin twigs. They will radiate from each corner of the opening. Begin by cutting an angle in the end of the twig so it will fit in the 90 degree angle of the corner. Cut one side…

..and the other.

Start with the center of the corner. Line it up with the grain. This is the longest ray.

The outer ray in the corner is the shortest. Cut one and eyeball the rest. Notice that the angle you cut in the end is much sharper than the center ray.

When nailing the rays in place, the nails should make a pattern and become one of the decorative elements.

Continue the rays into the adjoining segments.

Places where small branches were cut off can be touched up. This is a Guardsman touch-up pen. Before. ....After.

Continue to the other corners for this result.

Place the mirror or glass in the opening.

Add a backing piece...

...and secure

Use a nail to make a pilot for the eye screw.   Insert a eye screw.

Sign your frame.

A Three-Legged Table

Skye Gregson was born in the Adirondacks in October, 1983. As a Gregson, she was immediately exposed to this artistic family. Her dad was already widely recognized throughout the U.S. as one of the leading rustic artists. She grew up with this furniture and thought each piece was made for her personal pleasure.

She immediately took to the art form at a very young age. At the age of four, Skye was insisting that her brothers, Matthew and Dylan, get off the shaving horse, so she could do that too! Her dad was then inspired to build one just her size. From day one she has always been detail oriented, so this made rustic and all the work and details involved right up her alley.

She joined her dad at the Adirondack Museum, when he was asked to demonstrate old time tools and techniques used in making rustic furniture. Even as a very young girl she assisted him with live demos at many museums, libraries, arts councils, and community events around the region. At the age of eight, she was hired by the Adirondack Museum to demonstrate in their education building. They later hired her to demonstrate and represent the Museum in Albany and at other locations.

When Skye turned 12, she was invited as a speaker for the Northeastern Woodworkers Association, demonstrating old-time toy making. She was invited back for many years and the Association eventually challenged her to make her own chair for the competitions. She took second place in the chair category, competing with the professionals from the entire Northeast.

During this show, Roy Underhill, star of "The Woodwrights Shop" on television, visited with Skye and asked if he could film her for his show. He showed up with the complete film crew and they all did a fantastic show. "Making Rustic Chairs with Skye Gregson."

Skye continues to build chairs by order and for Adirondack Rustics Gallery in Schroon Lake, New York, owned and operated by Barry & Darlene Gregson.

Her commissioned works are in the permanent collections of the Shelburne Museum, Shelburne, Vermont, and the Adirondack Museum, Blue Mountain Lake, New York.

The wood is harvested at least a year before use. For pieces that will have the bark on we harvest in November. This is apple, so, even though I will be stripping the bark, November harvested wood will have better color.

I use a burnisher to rub off the bark. The blade is curved and blunt.

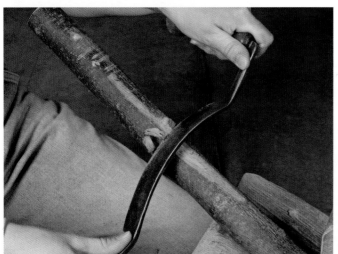

I go down to the cambium layer.

When you bust through, this nice brown color will begin to appear. This layer gives the smoothest surface.

Progress.

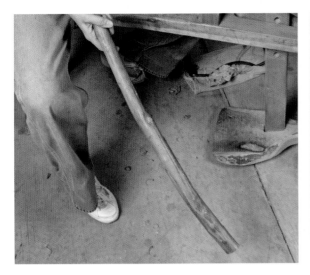

Continue until the surface is revealed.

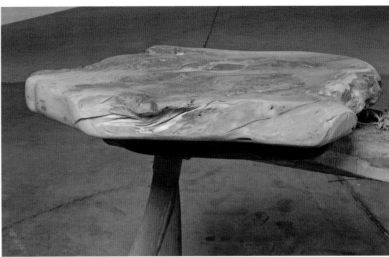

The table top is cherry burl. It needs to be at least 2" thick. If there is dead or rotten wood on the outside knock it off with your finger or a mallet.

Some sap wood at the edge (the lighter bands) is okay, but it is softer so shouldn't go more than 2" into the wood.

Rough sand the wood to 150 grit.

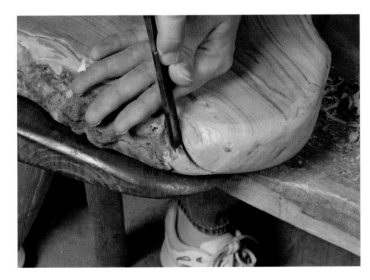

I like the natural cracks. A beveled gouge opens up the sides of the crack.

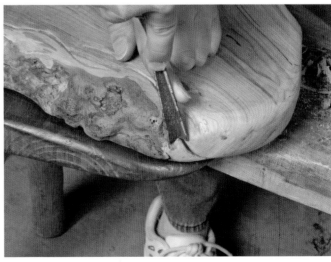

To go deeper, use a v-tool.

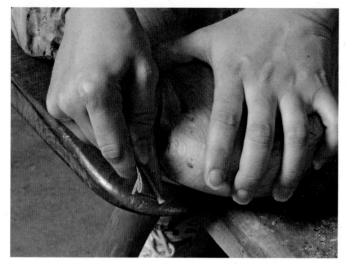

Go into the cracks and smooth with sand paper.

Continue with the deeper cracks.

Sand the top to 320 grit.

After burnishing the legs go over them with 320 grit paper.

Make a 1" diameter, 3/4" tenon on the top end of the leg. Keep the end of the leg close to the clamp so it has more stability. I am using a tenon cutter with a hand brace.

The result.

Decide the pitch of the first leg.

The height at the desired pitch should be at least 25-1/2". This will give a 26" table height.

With the leg in position, draw the level line around of the foot.

Cut it off. Rough cut all the legs to the same length and pitch.

Use a disc sander to round the edges.

Number the bottoms of the legs.

Stand the legs (a rubber band around their tops may help) and hold the top to visualize their final positions.

Now turn the top over and reposition the legs where they will go.

With each leg, draw a circle around the tenon.

Mark the circle with the leg number. Continue with the second leg...

...and the third, keeping the tenons close together.

Mark each circle with a leg number.

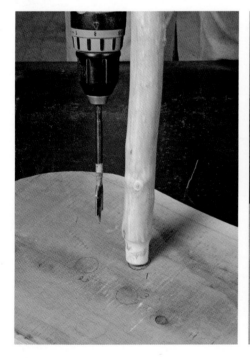

Hold the leg in place and visualize the angle of the mortise.

Align the drill to the correct angle.

Drill the mortise. Use a 1" drill bit for the 1" tenon. Don't go too deep...3/4" deep on a 2" thick top.

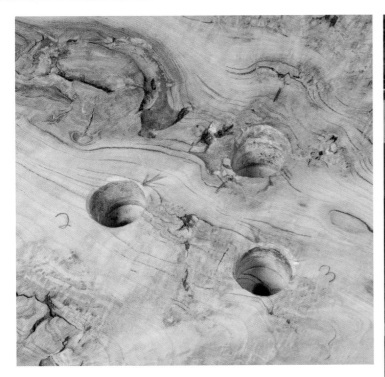

Repeat the process for the other two legs.

Rub a thin layer of wood glue on the tenon, and a bit in the mortise, then drive the legs in place for a rough fitting.

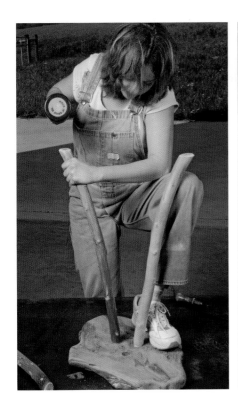

The second leg.

Eyeball the slope and alignment. Remove excess glue. I use wood chips for this.

Turn the table over to check for level. I check in two directions, lengthwise…

...and width-wise.

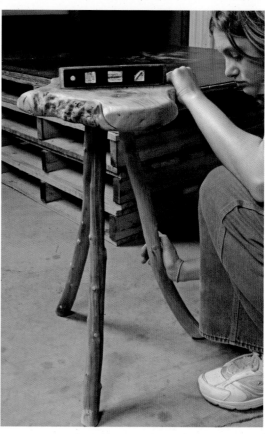

Leveling is a matter of pushing in if it needs to go up...

...or pulling out if it is too high.

Keep working it until you get to level.

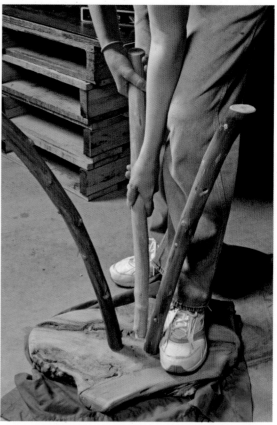

In this case I pounded leg #1 in too far, so I turn the table over and gently work the leg out a little.

This does the trick.

Recheck the level of the width as well.

Progress.

Find a visually appealing bent piece of wood that will also add some bracing. Ideally it will touch all three legs and come up to the side of the table top. The wood should have been harvested earlier, and be well-dried.

Test the position…

…until you find one that is just right.

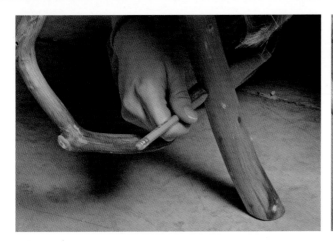

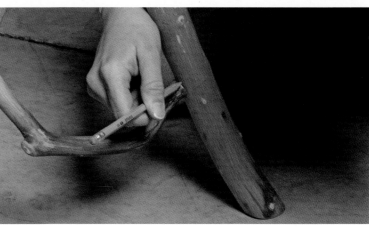

With the brace in place, mark the contact location where the end of the brace meets the leg…

…and the angle of the screw.

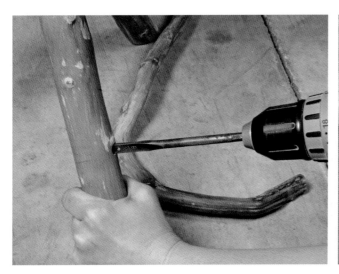

With a 3/8" bit, drill a countersink about 1/4" into the leg. Follow the angle you want for the screw.

Clamp the brace in place.

Countersink through the brace into the leg at the two touch-points.

Finally countersink into the table.

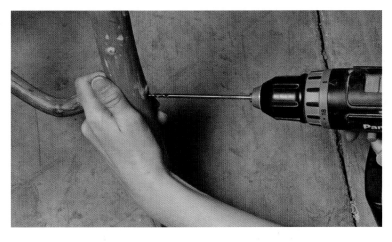

Enlarge the hole in the leg to allow the screw to turn freely. I use 5/32" bit for a No. 8 square head screw. Follow the angle the screw will follow. Go just slightly into the end of the brace.

Do the same at the other joints, going through the brace and slightly into the leg or top.

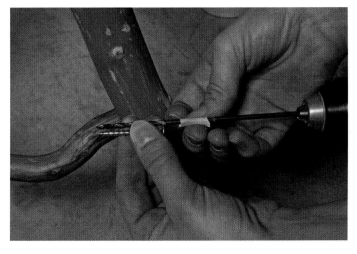

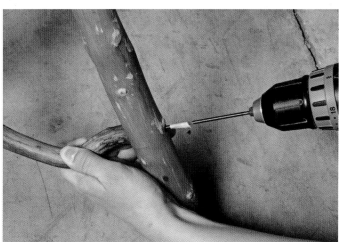

Finally make a pilot with 1/8" bit. Mark the depth on the bit with a piece of tape. It should be the length of the screw plus a bit more for the countersink.

Drill the hole.

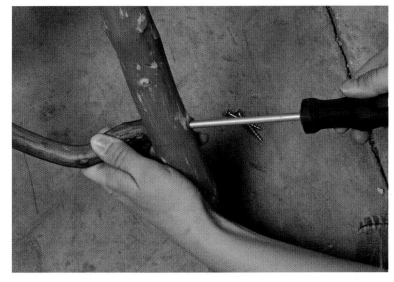

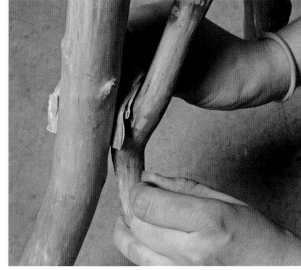

Screw in place.

If the drill created a burr, sand it away before screwing. You want a nice, flush joint.

Recheck for level.

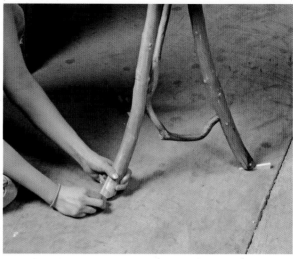

If there is a leveling problem, adjust it by using wedges under each foot.

Set a compass to the highest gap between the floor and the three legs.

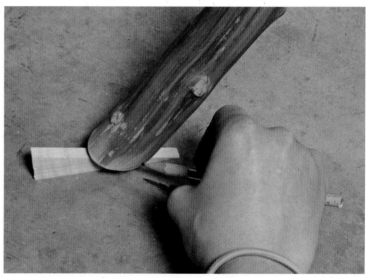

Use the compass as a depth gauge and carry the line around all three feet.

Reduce all the legs until they touch the line. You can use a disc sander for most adjustments.

Finishing may involve removing the branch nubs. I like to do it as one of the final steps, though others do it when burnishing.

For a finish I generously paint on a General Finishes product, Seal-A-Cel, which is mixture of polyurethane and tung oil. I use two brushes, rubber-banded together and work the finish into all the cracks and crevices.

Then I take a lint-free cotton bed sheet, ripped into pieces, and do a wet rub, vigorously rubbing the finish into the surface, especially the cracks and crevices, until I feel my hands getting hot.

This is followed by a dry buffing, also with a clean piece of the lint-free cotton. Again, I rub until my hands get hot.

The piece then sits overnight. The next day I use 0000 steel wool and go over the piece to remove any pithing or dust. If the surface will be used for glasses or food, I repeat the process three times.

Marcia Perry Marcia Perry Ma

Marcia Perry Marcia Perry Ma

A Child's Chair

Marcia Perry describes herself as a sculptor of trees. She spent her early years in the northern woods of Michigan surrounded by their "soft presence."

Her first experience of carving was at the age of 17, when she carved an ashtray. Enchanted by the process, she soon was carving other things—birds, bowls, weedpots. Her carvings helped finance her college education, which led to a varied career path, including corporate management, freelance writing, and poetry.

But the desire to carve never left her. At 37, she decided to devote a year of her life to making art. It was then that "miracles began occurring," as she describes it. "Opportunities appeared, possibilities expanded, dreams grew large—and most satisfying of all, the trees revealed themselves to me in a happy variety of shapes and character." (From her book, *For the Love of Trees*, © 2004.)

Her work can be seen at The Ark Gallery in Saugatuck, Michigan, as well as a few select mid-western galleries. Her work is part of private and public collections in Australia, Canada, the Czech Republic, France, Great Britain, and various sites across the United States.

The child's seat will be carved from this log. The log should have enough diameter to contain a comfortable seat surrounded by a wall. It should be tall enough to have a canopy. This is a nice piece of locust, a very hard wood suitable for use inside or outdoors.

Examine the log carefully and try to envision where and how the seat should be situated. Look at all sides before making your decision.

Then mark the top of the seat. An adult seat is about 17-18 inches from the ground. For this little child's seat it should be about 10-12 inches, (depending on the size of the child you have in mind for it.).

Next define the seat opening. I don't like to have it be symmetrical, but this is the maker's option.

If you come to an obstacle, like this knot, that may become problematic around the opening, carry the line around it.

Clearly mark the area to be removed.

For ease of work I like to lean the log back, giving me a more accessible angle.

Be sure to carefully wedge it in place, you don't want it moving while you are chainsawing.

Adjust the tension on your chainsaw blade. There should be a little give (1/4 inch or so) when you lift the chain. I use a Stihl 180 because it has a good weight/power ratio. It is equipped with a 12" "quarter tip" carving bar. There is also a finer "dime tip" bar for detail work that requires a different (1/4" pitch) chain and sprocket.

Start cutting slightly above the seat line from one direction...

...and make a flat cut.

Pivot the saw from the middle of the log to gain more depth, making sure the blade does not pierce through the back or sidewalls.

It may help to envision the rounded shape of the back of the chair's alcove.

Cut back along the same kerf in the other direction.

Cut vertically (rip) along the left edge of the alcove.

Plunge the bar about half way in...

Then repeat to deepen the cut.

Define the top of the alcove by cutting a wedge. Begin by cutting down from the apex, following the lines you have drawn until it meets the edge cut.

Next move a little lower and cut straight in to make a wedge.

Pivot the bar to deepen this bottom cut, always keeping in mind the round back of the alcove.

This angle provides an opportunity to deepen the bottom cut.

Turn the log as needed for better access.

Cut the other edge.

At the corner, connect the two cuts.

The result.

Rip a cut straight down the middle of the soon-to-be-opening.

Deepen the cut.   Connect the cuts at the corners.

Use a wedge or crow bar to pry the chunk of wood loose.

This long-handled wedge provides good leverage.

Where the wood is holding, cut it free.

Continue working until the wood pops out.

Do the same on the other side–cutting...

...and prying...

...until the piece comes loose.

The result.

Resituate the log to a comfortable working position.

We want to make the back deeper and give it a nice curve. Begin by making 1-3" deep horizontal cuts across the inside surface.

Then trim with the grain along the edges.

Continue around the top of the alcove.

Deepen the crosscuts.

Drive a wedge between the now-defined segments...

...then work around the edges to pry them loose.

Loosen as much as you can with the wedge...

...then remove the splinters with a chisel.

Hollowing out the cavity of the log is simply a patient process of using the chainsaw to cut the depth...

...the wedge to loosen the pieces...

...the chisel for clean up...

...and hands to remove the unwanted wood.

Progress.

Ergonomically, you may find it much more comfortable to put the log on a sturdy table. It takes a lot of pressure off your back. Also, be sure to wear safety equipment at all times.

Continue to shape the recess.

The end of the saw can be used to help in the shaping, but it leaves a rough texture.

When the general shape of the opening is satisfactory, you can start finer smoothing. A wide gouge is used to shape the back of the seat where it joins the walls. This transition should be a gentle slope.

Even in this refining stage, the chainsaw is useful for shaping...

...in combination with the chisel.

The back still needs to be deeper, so it is scored with some more chainsaw lines...

...then cleaned up with a chisel.

The removal of all this material does require patience. The goal here is to have a thin wall all around the alcove.

This small, electric chainsaw is lightweight and very maneuverable. It can be used as an alternative for material removal.

You may also try an electric grinder.

It is a good time to check your progress. Bare hands are best to feel if there are areas needing more work

The grinding does add some surface texture, but less than the chain cutters. With power tools at this stage, you must be careful not to be too aggressive.

To contour the seat, return to the gas chainsaw.

For comfort, the seat should curve gently down toward the back and center. The ideal sitting position is with the knees higher than the hips.

The edges should have that same curve.

Shape the seat bottom.

Progress.

Clean up the seat, cutting down high points with the gouge and mallet. Continue this combination of chainsaw and gouge until you like the shape.

There should be a smooth slope between the seat and the walls.

Continue smoothing the walls. Your goal is an integrated surface with no hard corners.

The top of the log was not flat, but had a raised portion. This offers the opportunity for an interesting feature. For now, I just want to define it a bit more. Trim this side...

...and the other. I'll return to this later.

With the rough shaping completed, it is time to start the finishing work with abrasives. Begin with an aggressive sander.

Be sure to wear a respirator, ear protection, goggles, gloves, and appropriate protective clothes.

The goal is to smooth the whole interior of the chair until it is smooth as the baby's bottom which is intended to sit in it. Start with low number abrasives and proceed to higher (finer) sandpapers. I usually use #36 (briefly), 60, 80 or100, 150, 220, 320, 400 grit.

This is very dusty work, so you may need to change the respirator's filter along the way.

When one round of sanding is complete, change to a finer grit and a softer pad. This will allow you to smooth and shape the rounded contours of the log.

Soften the edges.

Work your way into the sides....

...the seat...

...the top.

...the back...

Progress.

We can now return to the decorative piece on the top, which was defined earlier.

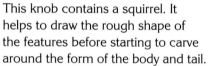

This knob contains a squirrel. It helps to draw the rough shape of the features before starting to carve around the form of the body and tail.

The bushy tail will wrap around the outside. Use a v-tool or a deep sweep gouge to separate the body from the tail.

Gradually deepen the separation between the tail and the body.

Shape the body and head, leaving plenty of wood for the ears.

Gradually, the figure will emerge from the wood.

Return to the sander for some finish work inside the alcove.

An animal carving adds a great deal of interest to a chair.

With the chair upright and the carving nearly finished, you can also refine the top of the chair.

Soften the edges, blending them into the sides.

With great care, you can also smooth the carving.

A willing volunteer has been found to "test ride" the chair. The fit is pretty good.

With a little more fine sanding (220-400 grit), the chair is ready for an application of finish.

In a container, make a 50-50 mix of the two ingredients. (It will penetrate faster if it is heated up to the point where vapors rise, but this step is optional.)

The treatment I use is a mixture of boiled linseed oil and gum turpentine.

Using a clean cloth, apply the finish to the interior of the chair. This is when the rich color and patterns of grain emerge.

I usually apply it to the base of the chair as well. Even though it won't be seen, it protects the wood.

Coat the sides of the chair...

...and the top.

Work the finish into the nooks and crannies of the sculptural carving with a brush and oil saturated rag. Squirrels love a good massage!

Go back over the piece to be sure the coverage is complete. When dry, apply again. Be sure to wipe off any excess oil, as it can dry and become gummy. Wiping down with a cotton cloth prevents this and should help the sanded surfaces gleam.

The completed chair. Locust wood is suitable
for indoor or outdoor use. If placed in the sun,
be aware that the colors will fade over time and
the surfaces may appear silvery-gray.

Marcia's Gallery

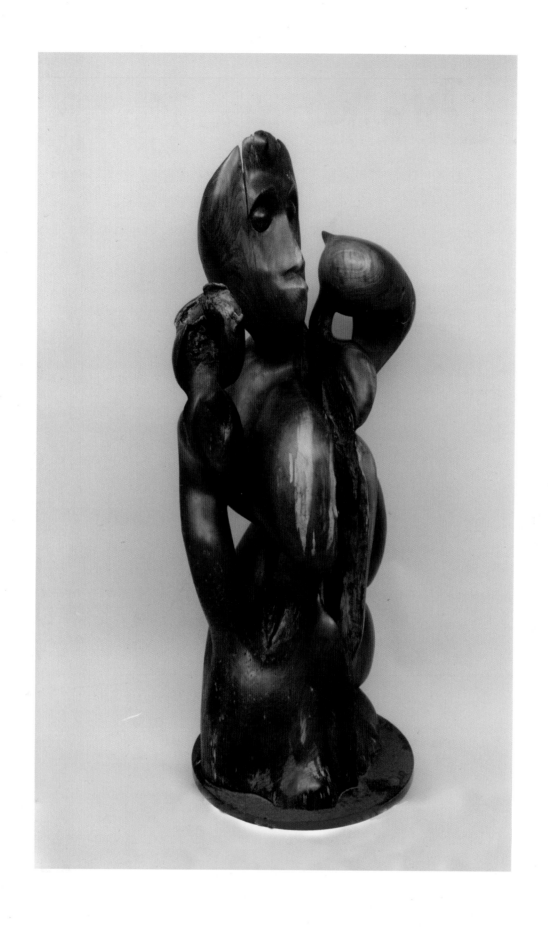